on Word Work

Word Work

Book 2

**Louis Fidge and
Sarah Lindsay**

FOCUS on Word Work

Using this book

This book will help you to understand words better. It will help you to develop good spelling strategies, teach you useful spelling rules and extend your vocabulary.

What's in a unit

Each unit is set out in the same way as the example here. There are also Progress Units to help you check how well you are doing.

Unit heading
This tells you what you will be learning about

The rule
This explains the rule and gives an example

More to think about
Activities to practise and develop your understanding

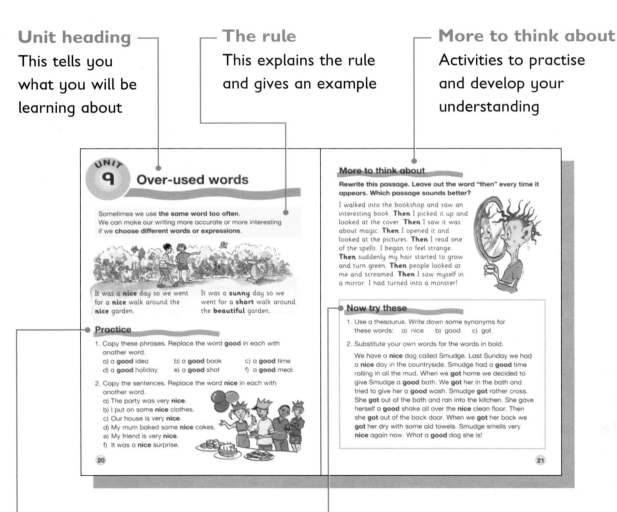

UNIT 9 — Over-used words

Sometimes we use **the same word too often**. We can make our writing more accurate or more interesting if we **choose different words or expressions**.

It was a **nice** day so we went for a **nice** walk around the **nice** garden.

It was a **sunny** day so we went for a **short** walk around the **beautiful** garden.

Practice

1. Copy these phrases. Replace the word **good** in each with another word.
   a) a **good** idea   b) a **good** book   c) a **good** time
   d) a **good** holiday   e) a **good** shot   f) a **good** meal

2. Copy the sentences. Replace the word **nice** in each with another word.
   a) The party was very **nice**.
   b) I put on some **nice** clothes.
   c) Our house is very **nice**.
   d) My mum baked some **nice** cakes.
   e) My friend is very **nice**.
   f) It was a **nice** surprise.

20

More to think about

Rewrite this passage. Leave out the word "then" every time it appears. Which passage sounds better?

I walked into the bookshop and saw an interesting book. **Then** I picked it up and looked at the cover. **Then** I saw it was about magic. **Then** I opened it and looked at the pictures. **Then** I read one of the spells. I began to feel strange. **Then** suddenly my hair started to grow and turn green. **Then** people looked at me and screamed. **Then** I saw myself in a mirror. I had turned into a monster!

Now try these

1. Use a thesaurus. Write down some synonyms for these words: a) nice   b) good   c) got

2. Substitute your own words for the words in bold.

   We have a **nice** dog called Smudge. Last Sunday we had a **nice** day in the countryside. Smudge had a **good** time rolling in all the mud. When we **got** home we decided to give Smudge a **good** bath. We **got** her in the bath and tried to give her a **good** wash. Smudge **got** rather cross. She **got** out of the bath and ran into the kitchen. She gave herself a **good** shake all over the **nice** clean floor. Then she **got** out of the back door. When we **got** her back we **got** her dry with some old towels. Smudge smells very **nice** again now. What a **good** dog she is!

21

Practice
Activities to practise and check your understanding

Now try these
Activities to stretch and extend your understanding

Contents

A **definition** is the **meaning** of a word.

Dinosaurs were huge animals that roamed the Earth a long time ago.

This is how Gurdip defines dinosaurs.

Dinosaurs were large reptiles that lived in prehistoric times.

This is a **dictionary definition** of dinosaurs.

Dinosaurs – large prehistoric reptiles.

This is an even shorter way of defining dinosaurs.

Practice

Use a dictionary to help you.

These words and definitions have got mixed up. Write the correct definition for each word.

1. centipede   a house built on one level only

2. yak   the woolly coat from a sheep

3. bungalow   a small crawling insect with many legs

4. monastery   a large number of musicians who play music together

5. quiver   a long-haired ox from the Himalayas

6. architect   a case for holding arrows

7. fleece   someone who plans and designs new buildings

8. orchestra   a place where monks live and work

More to think about

Write your own definitions for the following words.

1. weigh   2. swim   3. purse   4. medicine

6. encyclopedia   7. anchor   8. hangar

5. fog

Now compare your definitions with those given in a dictionary!

Now try these

Re-write these dictionary definitions. Use as few words as possible.

1. panda   The giant panda is a rare, black and white, bear-like animal which lives in the bamboo forests of China.

    panda –   a rare, black and white animal from China

2. aviary   An aviary is a large outdoor cage for keeping birds.

3. vaccinate   When a doctor vaccinates you, he or she injects you with a medicine to protect you from disease.

4. aspirin   This is a drug made into a tablet which is used to treat headaches and minor pains.

5. desert   A desert is a dry wasteland where few things grow.

6. dessert   A dessert is a sweet or a pudding eaten after the main course.

Syllables

Syllables are the **beats** in a word.

Read the word **bubble** aloud.
Now read it very slowly...   **bub/ble**
The word **bub/ble** has two **syllables**.

bubble

bar/row

drum/mer

These words also have two **syllables**.
Each **syllable** must contain at least one vowel.

Practice

Copy the words that have two syllables.

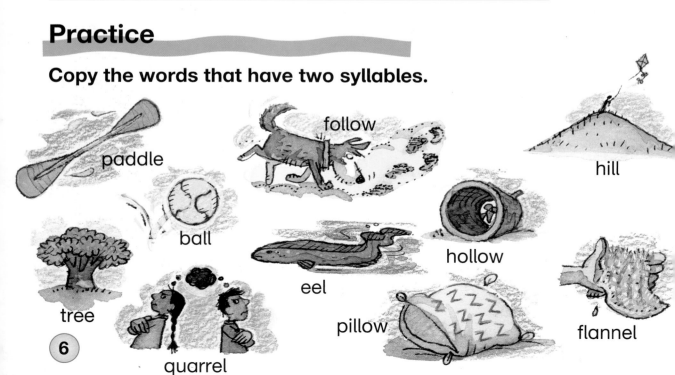

paddle

follow

hill

ball

tree

hollow

eel

flannel

quarrel

pillow

More to think about

Copy the words. Draw a line between the double consonants to separate the syllables.

1. puppet pup/pet
2. shallow
3. funnel
4. attract
5. fillet
6. minnow
7. bullet
8. vessel
9. narrow
10. attack
11. kennel
12. arrow

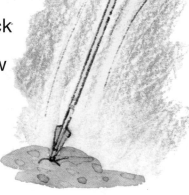

Now try these

1. The answers to these clues all have two syllables.
   Fill in the missing double consonants.

   a) A colour   ye ___ ___ ow

   b) A loud shout   be ___ ___ ow

   c) A rabbit lives in one   bu ___ ___ ow

   d) A little bird   spa ___ ___ ow

   e) To get somewhere   a ___ ___ ive

   f) A type of tree   wi ___ ___ ow

2. Think of five more words that have two syllables and
   double consonants. Write a clue for each word.

Alphabetical order
(third and fourth letter)

To arrange words in **alphabetical order** you look at the first letters in the words. If the first and second letters in the words are the same, you have to look at the **third or fourth letters** to arrange them in **alphabetical order**.

I've got a bad code!

co**d**e   co**l**d   co**r**k   co**s**t

These words are arranged in **alphabetical order** according to the third letter.

com**b**   com**e**t   com**i**c   com**p**uter

These words are arranged in **alphabetical order** according to the fourth letter.

Practice

1. Arrange these words in alphabetical order according to the third letter.
   a) badger, baby, basin, ball
   b) acorn, acrobat, accident, ache
   c) pear, penguin, pebble, peck

2. Arrange these words in alphabetical order according to the fourth letter
   a) bear, beaver, beak, bead
   b) cheese, chestnut, chemist, cherry
   c) shop, shoe, shore, shoot

More to think about

1. Write the word that comes *after* each of these words in your dictionary.

   a) bulb   b) glitter   c) portrait

   d) rust   e) crumple   f) famous

   g) metal   h) roof

2. Write the word that comes *before* each of these words in your dictionary.

   a) ripe   b) usual   c) vandal

   d) idle   e) currant   f) kettle

   g) purr   h) wharf

Now try these

Use the definitions to help you find these words in your dictionary.

1. la _ _ _ _ _ _ _ _ _   a room where scientists work

   la _ _   a long string to fasten your shoes

   la _ _ _   a large spoon with a long handle for serving soup

   la _ _ _ _ _ _ _   words we use when speaking or writing

   la _ _   volcanic rock that is red hot

2. sha _ _   an area of darkness not reached by the sun

   sha _ _ _   with long, thick, untidy hair

   sha _ _ _ _   not deep

   sha _ _ _ _   liquid for washing hair

   sha _ _ _ _   break suddenly into small pieces

UNIT 4 — Homophones

Homophones are words that **sound the same** but have **different spellings and meanings**.

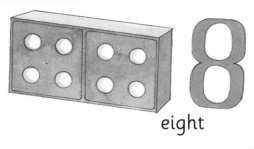

eight

ate

Say the words **eight** and **ate** aloud.
They sound the same.
They are **spelt differently** and have **different meanings**.

Practice

Write the correct homophone to match the picture.

1.    **dough** or **doe**

2.    **sure** or **shore**

3.   **write** or **right**

4.    **ruff** or **rough**

5.    **stair** or **stare**

Use a dictionary to help you.

More to think about

1. Copy the sentence. Choose the correct homophone.
   a) Rakesh wasn't sure (weather / whether) to have another sweet.
   b) "I can't (hear / here) you," shouted the man.
   c) Emma and Lee couldn't (weight / wait) until Christmas.
   d) Stuart (through / threw) the ball so hard it went over the school fence!
   e) The bus (fare / fair) was £2.50.
   f) "(Witch / which) picture is mine?" asked Kathy.

2. Copy, from above, the homophones you haven't used. Write a sentence for each one.

Now try these

1. Write your own definition for each of the words in the boxes. Use your dictionary to help if you need to.

saw	rain	road	vein
sore	reign	rowed	vane
soar	rein	rode	vain

2. Write a sentence that has **to**, **two** and **too** in it.

3. Write a sentence that has **they're**, **there** and **their** in it.

Rhyming

> I **wish** I had a **fish** in a **dish**.

> Don't **chew** my best **blue shoe**!

Sometimes **rhyming** words contain the **same** letter patterns.	Sometimes **rhyming** words sound alike but have **different** letter patterns.

Practice

Match the rhyming words. Write them in pairs.

1.

sway	five
fly	tall
drive	tray
small	see
tree	cry

2.

shine	alarm
farm	measure
above	wriggle
giggle	fine
treasure	glove

More to think about

1. Match each word in Set A with its rhyming word in Set B.

Set A	learn	boot	chalk	take	plain
	purse	hate	store	boat	sneeze

Set B	squawk	wrote	please	burn	straight
	break	verse	raw	cane	suit

2. Copy these words. Underline the odd word in each set.
   a) post cost lost frost   b) moth both cloth broth
   c) rough tough enough cough   d) mice twice nice office
   e) cart start wart dart   f) meat great seat beat

Now try these

1. These clues are answered with pairs of rhyming words.
   Fill in the gap with the second rhyming word.
   a) a joyful race = fun _____run_____
   b) a young hen that is ill = sick _____
   c) a fizzy drink store = pop _____
   d) a conceited horse rider = cocky _____
   e) blond locks = fair _____
   f) recipe collection = cook _____
   g) an angry employer = cross _____

2. Write two sentences for each pair of homonyms to
   show you know the different meanings of the words.
   a) bough/bow   b) root/route
   c) serial/cereal   d) aisle/isle
   e) waist/waste   f) profit/prophet
   g) fined/find   h) bare/bear

Verbs: s, ed and ing endings

A **verb** is an action word.

If **ed** is added to a verb it means the action has already happened in the **past**.

If **s** or **ing** is added to a verb it means the action is happening in the **present**.

whispered

whispers   whispering

Tess **whispered** to her friend.

Tess **whispers** to her friend.

Tess is **whispering** to her friend.

If **ing** or **ed** is added to a verb ending in **e**, the **e** is dropped.

stumble **+** **ing** = stumbl**ing**
stumble **+** **ed** = stumbl**ed**

Practice

Copy and fill in this table.

Verb	Past (add **ed**)	Present (add **s**)	Present (add **ing**)
cook	cooked	cooks	cooking
climb			
howl			
shout			
kick			
comb			

More to think about

1. Copy the sentences. Write the correct verb endings (**ed**, **s**, **ing**) to fill in the gap.

   a) Titus scream_____ when he saw the ghost. (*Past*)

   b) The old, frail man is walk_____ his dog by the canal. (*Present*)

   c) Kevin shout_____ loudly at his friends, while playing football. (*Present*)

   d) The wind is blow_____ down the valley. (*Present*)

   e) The farmer climb_____ over the gate to reach his cows. (*Past*)

2. Write a sentence for each word in the box.

screams	walked	shouting	blows	climbs

Now try these

1. Copy and fill in the table.

	+ing	+ s	+ed
argue			
scream			
mumble			
squeal			
grumble			

2. The words in the first column above are ways people communicate. Choose two of the words. Write three sentences using the different endings for each word. Make your sentences interesting.

Suffixes (1)

A **suffix** is a group of letters added to the **end** of a word to change its meaning or the way it can be used.

A **suffix** can sometimes change an adjective into a verb.

sharp ⟶ **sharpen**

A **suffix** can sometimes change a noun into a verb.

plan ⟶ **planned**

Practice

1. Add the suffix **en** to change these adjectives into verbs.
   Write the verbs.

   a) black_en_ blacken   b) quick____

   c) soft____   d) dark____   e) sharp____

   f) sweet____   g) short____   h) tight____

2. Copy these verbs. Underline the adjectives from which
   they are made.

   a) <u>brigh</u>ten   b) sadden   c) lengthen   d) <u>d</u>ea<u>den</u>

   e) soften   f) broaden   g) fatten   h) widen

More to think about

1. Copy the table. Write the verbs in the box in the correct columns.

| magnetise | handle | sparkle | advertise | trample |
| fossilise | equalise | startle | curdle | specialise |

ise words	**le** words

2. Write the verbs above. Write the root word each came from.

   magnetise – magnet

Now try these

1. Copy these verbs. Write the root word from which each verb comes.

   a) apologise – apology   b) simplify

   c) memorise   d) liquidate   e) glorify

   f) dramatise   g) purify   h) motivate

2. Choose four of the verbs above. Write a sentence for each one that shows you know its meaning.

Sorry!

UNIT 8 Verbs: irregular past tenses

When we write a **regular verb** in the **past** tense, the **root word stays the same**.

scream   screamed

When we write an **irregular verb** in the **past** tense, the **root word changes**.

drink    drank

Practice

Copy these sentences. Write the word with the correct tense.

1. The seagulls (fly/flew) low over James' head as he throws them bread.
2. The class (write/wrote) the date on every piece of work they do.
3. "The choir (sing/sang) loudly and clearly last night," praised the teacher.
4. Matthew's nan (bring/brought) him a bike last Christmas.
5. Clare (go/went) to her best friend's house last Friday.
6. Malik's dad (write/wrote) a diary when he was a boy.
7. The Smith family (fly/flew) to America for their holiday.
8. "(Sing/Sang) quietly please, I'm trying to watch this programme," John said to his brother.
9. "Can we (go/went) now?" asked Tara.

More to think about

1. Copy the table. Fill in the missing verbs.

Present	Past
throw	threw
swim	
	stood
go	
drink	
	took
come	
	brought
	could
eat	

2. Think of four more irregular verbs to add to your table.

Now try these

Copy the sentences. Correct the tense of the underlined word.

1. The bottle fell off the table and <u>break</u>.
2. Mrs Seal <u>speak</u> quietly but firmly to the two girls.
3. The family <u>come</u> to the fair to enjoy the scary rides.
4. The two children <u>swam</u> 500 metres and raised £23.
5. Richard and Indira <u>take</u> their dog for a walk every day.
6. Kelly <u>do</u> her homework before she went out to play.
7. Aziz <u>eat</u> a pizza yesterday.

19

UNIT 9 Over-used words

Sometimes we use **the same word too often**.
We can make our writing more accurate or more interesting
if we **choose different words or expressions**.

It was a **nice** day so we went for a **nice** walk around the **nice** garden.

It was a **sunny** day so we went for a **short** walk around the **beautiful** garden.

Practice

1. Copy these phrases. Replace the word **good** in each with another word.

   a) a **good** idea
   b) a **good** book
   c) a **good** time
   d) a **good** holiday
   e) a **good** shot
   f) a **good** meal

2. Copy the sentences. Replace the word **nice** in each with another word.

   a) The party was very **nice**.
   b) I put on some **nice** clothes.
   c) Our house is very **nice**.
   d) My mum baked some **nice** cakes.
   e) My friend is very **nice**.
   f) It was a **nice** surprise.

More to think about

Rewrite this passage. Leave out the word "then" every time it appears. Which passage sounds better?

I walked into the bookshop and saw an interesting book. **Then** I picked it up and looked at the cover. **Then** I saw it was about magic. **Then** I opened it and looked at the pictures. **Then** I read one of the spells. I began to feel strange. **Then** suddenly my hair started to grow and turn green. **Then** people looked at me and screamed. **Then** I saw myself in a mirror. I had turned into a monster!

Now try these

1. Use a thesaurus. Write down some synonyms for these words: a) nice   b) good   c) got

2. Substitute your own words for the words in bold.

   We have a **nice** dog called Smudge. Last Sunday we had a **nice** day in the countryside. Smudge had a **good** time rolling in all the mud. When we **got** home we decided to give Smudge a **good** bath. We **got** her in the bath and tried to give her a **good** wash. Smudge **got** rather cross. She **got** out of the bath and ran into the kitchen. She gave herself a **good** shake all over the **nice** clean floor. Then she **got** out of the back door. When we **got** her back we **got** her dry with some old towels. Smudge smells very **nice** again now. What a **good** dog she is!

Suffixes (2)

A **suffix** is a group of letters added to the **end** of a word to change its meaning or the way it can be used.
Some common suffixes are **able**, **ible**, **tion** and **sion**.

sensible	miserable	division	direction

When adding **able** or **ible** to a word that ends in **e** you usually drop the **e**.

sense + ible = sensible

When adding **tion** or **sion** to a word that ends in **e** you usually **drop the e and the letter before it**.

explode + sion = explosion

Practice

Match the word with the correct picture.
Underline the suffix in each word.

explosion	instruction	invisible	valuable	sensible	operation

1.

2.

3.

4.

5.

6.

More to think about

Add the suffixes to these words.

1. pollute   +   tion   =   pollution
2. decide   +   sion   =
3. love   +   able   =
4. sense   +   ible   =
5. educate   +   tion   =
6. recognise   +   able   =
7. collide   +   sion   =
8. believe   +   able   =

Now try these

1. Copy the table. Write the words in the box in the correct columns.

forcible	believable	invasion	explosion
subtraction	instruction	invisible	imagination
division	responsible	valuable	agreeable

ible	able	sion	tion

2. Add three more words of your own to each column.

3. Choose two words from each column. Write a sentence that includes both words, like this:

The **instruction** on how to do the **subtraction** sum wasn't very clear.

Progress Test A

1. Copy these words. Write the correct definition with each word.

cabin	not heavy, easy to lift
hospital	soft shoes worn indoors
light	a building where ill people are cared for
saddle	a small room on a ship
slippers	a seat on a horse

2. Write down the two-syllable words that can be made.

a) cur
   lor
   fer   ry
   mar

b) med
   fid
   cud   dle
   pad

c) pat
   bet
   fit   ter
   hot

3. Write these words in alphabetical order.
   seed   separate   season   selfish   second   send

4. Write the correct word for each picture.

hair hare	ball bawl	break brake	pale pail

5. Copy these rhyming words. Write another word to go with each pair.
   a) pair, wear   b) date, great   c) coat, note
   d) come, thumb   e) here, steer   f) learn, turn

6. Copy the table. Add **s**, **ing** and **ed** to these verbs.

	+s	+ing	+ed
kick			
hope			
wait			
wipe			
fill			

Take care with the spellings.

7. Copy these words. Write each word without its suffix.
   a) sharpen
   b) lengthen
   c) handle
   d) sparkle
   e) magnetise
   f) trample
   g) quicken
   h) legalise

8. Copy the sentences. Write each one again as if it happened yesterday.
   a) I drink some water.   Yesterday I drank some water.
   b) I catch a ball.   c) I go to school.   d) I blow a whistle.
   e) I leave home.   f) I tread on some ice.   g) I tear my coat.

9. Rewrite each sentence. Change the word in **bold** for a better word.
   a) I **got** home late.
   b) She **got** very angry.
   c) Sunday was a **nice** day.
   d) I had a **nice** lunch.
   e) The cake was **good**.
   f) I had a **good** sleep.

10. The suffixes on these words have got mixed up. Write the words correctly.

   a) comfortible   b) instrucsion   c) invisable   d) explotion

Gender

The **gender** of a person or an animal is either **masculine** (male) or **feminine** (female).

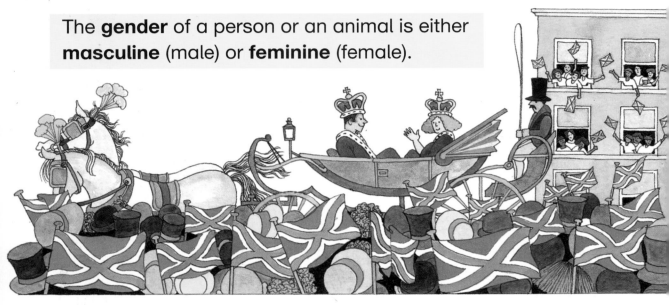

The queen waved to the crowds. The king sat and smiled.

The word **queen** is **feminine**. The word **king** is **masculine**.

Practice

Copy these sets of words. Join the two words that make a pair with a line.

1.

feminine	masculine
mother	brother
sister	nephew
daughter	uncle
aunt	father
niece	son

2.

feminine	masculine
cow	tiger
lioness	bull
hen	lion
tigress	drake
duck	cock

More to think about

1. Add the suffix **ess** to these masculine words to make them feminine. Write the word.
   a) baron baroness   b) count
   c) host   d) heir   e) manager
   f) mayor   g) lion   h) giant

2. Copy these words. Write (m) beside the word if it is masculine or (f) if it is feminine. Use a dictionary if necessary.
   a) grandmother   b) duchess   c) bridegroom
   d) goddess   e) monk   f) lord
   g) mare   h) ewe   i) vixen
   j) widow   k) gander   l) prince

3. Now write the opposite to each of the words above.

   a) grandmother — grandfather

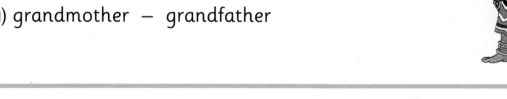

Now try these

Copy these sentences. Change the words in bold into the opposite.

1. The **princess** rode a horse. The prince rode a horse.
2. The **cow** was grazing in the meadow.
3. The **landlord** of the hotel was very helpful.
4. The **fox** was in the woods.
5. The **duchess** put on **her** best clothes.
6. The **bride** arrived early. **She** came by car.
7. The **lion** roared loudly in the bush.
8. Hissing angrily, the **goose** flapped to the gate.

al as a prefix and suffix

al often stands for the word **all**.

together

altogether

music   musical

The prefix **al** added to a word means **everyone** or **everything**.

The suffix **al** sounds very similar to the **el** and **le** endings of words, so you have to be careful when adding it.

If the word **ends** in **ic** the suffix **al** is used.

Practice

Add al to the beginning or end of these letters to complete the word.

1.

accident

2.

most

3.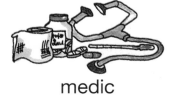

comic

4.

tropic

5.

right

6.

sign

7.

historic

8.

medic

More to think about

If you don't know the meaning of a word remember to look it up in a dictionary.

Write some sentences about a school visit.
Use all the al words in the box below.

altogether	accidental	historical	alright	although
	factual	always	mechanical	almost

Now try these

1. Copy the table. Some of these words are misspelt.
   Correct the words that are wrong.

Check the spellings in a dictionary if you need to.

al... (prefix)	...al (suffix)
allright	mechanicall
allthough	occasionall
altogether	medicall
allso	accidental
almighty	comical

2. Add two more words to the lists:
   a) beginning with **al**   b) ending with **al**.

Our living language

Our **language changes** all the time.
Words die out and new words come in.

The way we say things changes **over a period of time**.

Practice

Copy this list of words. Underline the words that you think have entered our language only in the last fifty years.

a) astronaut   b) supermarket   c) cart
d) light   e) computer   f) glass
g) farm   h) video   i) rain
j) refrigerator   k) radio   l) pencil

More to think about

Use a dictionary to help.

1. Copy the old words in Set A. Next to each word write the word in Set B that means the same.

Set A	frock omnibus perambulator butt quaff kin spectacles bonnet satchel pitcher

Set B	glasses pram drink dress bus barrel schoolbag relatives hat jug

2. Write these words. Match each word with its definition.
   Use a dictionary if necessary.

   a) **cobbler**   a measure of liquid

   b) **guinea**   a sitting-room

   c) **quart**   an old English coin

   d) **scuttle**   a cup for drinking out of

   e) **parlour**   someone who mends shoes

   f) **tinker**   food

   g) **goblet**   a container for coal

   h) **victuals**   someone who mends pots and pans

Now try these

Try writing this conversation in modern English!

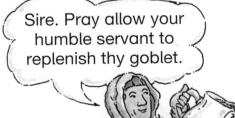

Sire. Pray allow your humble servant to replenish thy goblet.

Behold, thou careless varlet! My goblet runneth over onto my doublet. Get thee gone afore thou dost commit any more mischief.

Letter pattern: ight

One common letter pattern is **ight**.

I was fr**ight**ened by a noise in the n**ight**.

Practice

Match each word in the box with its picture.

fight	bright	light	tight	eight	fright

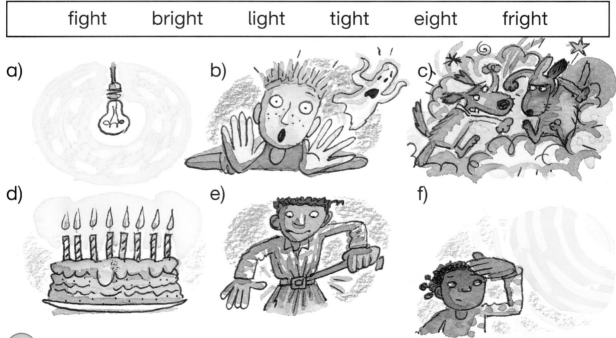

a)

b)

c)

d)

e)

f)

More to think about

Find eight ight words in this wordsearch.
Write a list of the words you find.

b	f	g	j	a	f	p
r	i	g	h	t	i	s
i	s	k	d	o	g	f
g	h	j	v	b	h	l
h	e	i	g	h	t	i
t	i	g	h	t	n	g
b	n	i	g	h	t	h
v	f	r	i	g	h	t

Now try these

1. Copy the sentences. Choose a word from the box to fill each gap.

brightly	fright	might	right	tightly
tonight		night		light

a) Ben held on _____ to his dad's hand.

b) The star shone _____.

c) Salma's friends _____ come to play.

d) The dog had a _____ when the fireworks were let off.

2. Four words in the box have not been used.
   Write four sentences each using one of these words.

UNIT 15 Suffixes (3)

I am interested in fashion.
I like fashionable clothes.

I like to invent things.
I am very inventive.

fashion ⟶ fashionable   invent ⟶ inventive

We can sometimes change a **noun** or a **verb** into an
adjective (a describing word) by adding a **suffix**.

Practice

Copy these words. Underline the root noun or verb in each.

a) musical   b) lucky   c) childish   d) comfortable
e) useful   f) heroic   g) dangerous   h) attractive
i) shocking   j) hopeful   k) faulty   l) pressing

More to think about

1. Choose which suffix to add to make these words into adjectives.

ous	al	y	ful

a) person___ b) help___ c) accident___ d) luck___

e) poison___ f) mountain___ g) thirst___ h) faith___

2. Choose which suffix to add to make these words into adjectives.

ish	ic	ing	able

a) angel___ b) wash___ c) boy___ d) exist___

e) tempt___ f) child___ g) girl___ h) depend___

Now try these

1. Copy these adjectives. Write the noun from which each of these adjectives comes.

   a) angry – anger   b) noisy   c) spotty

   d) adventurous   e) mysterious   f) natural

   g) criminal   h) beautiful   i) skilful

   j) energetic   k) gigantic   l) valuable

2. Copy these verbs. Change them into adjectives by adding the suffixes **ive**, **ent**, **ant** or **ous**.

   Take care with the spellings!

   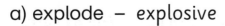

   a) explode – explosive

   b) obey   c) defy   d) prosper

   e) imagine   f) please   g) rebel

Common letter strings

These words have the **same letter patterns** but **different pronunciations**.

t**ough**   tr**ough**   thr**ough**

Say the words aloud.

Practice

Copy these words. Join the pairs of words with the same letter pattern.

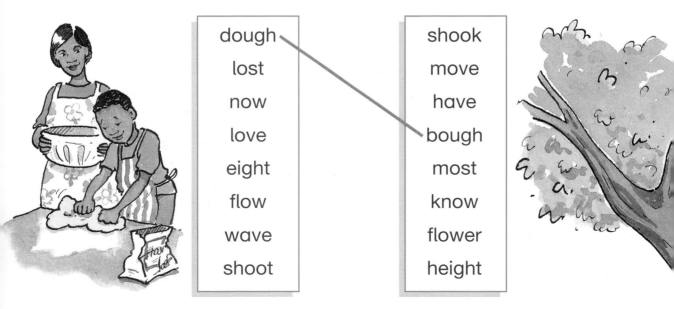

dough	shook
lost	move
now	have
love	bough
eight	most
flow	know
wave	flower
shoot	height

More to think about

1. Use the picture clue to find another word with the same letter pattern but a different pronunciation. Write the two words.

a) grown

b) vase

c) near

d) office

e) spine

f) gull

Use a dictionary if necessary.

2. Think of another word with the same letter pattern but a different pronunciation.
   a) g**oo**d   b) c**are**   c) c**aught**

Now try these

Write the two words in the same sentence.

1. eight/height
   By the age of **eight** Brian had grown to a **height** of one metre, thirty-five centimetres.

2. case/vase

3. flow/flower

4. cloth/mother

5. around/wound

6. dough/through

7. gone/stone

Compound words

A word which consists of **two smaller words** joined together is called a **compound word**.

book + mark = bookmark

cup + board = cupboard

Sometimes it is **easy** to hear how the word should be spelt when we say it.

Sometimes it is **hard** to hear how the word should be spelt when we say it.

Practice

Copy these word sums and write the compound words you make.

1. bull + dog = bulldog
2. butter + fly =
3. play + ground =
4. egg + cup =
5. arm + chair =
6. oat + cake =
7. table + cloth =
8. fire + work =

More to think about

Think of a compound word beginning with each of the
following words.

1. foot _____   2. door _____   3. tea _____

4. cross _____   5. back _____   6. butter _____

7. home _____   8. water _____   9. key _____

10. tooth _____   11. side _____   12. moon _____

Now try these

1. Copy these words. Join them to make compound words.

post   man   postcard

straw   bag

tomb   ache

hedge   stone

hand   card

tooth   berry

gentle   bin

dust   hog

2. Now underline the tricky bit in each
   compound word that is not pronounced.

   pos_t_card

Common root words

These words have the same **root word**.

tele**phone**

micro**phone**

phone

Practice

1. Copy the words. Underline the root word in each.

   a) farmer   farmyard

   b) shopper   shopping

   c) sunshine   sunlight

   d) lighthouse   candlelight

   e) football   barefoot

2. Explain why you think the root word was used in the words above, like this:

   farm   This root word was used in these words because a farmer works on a farm and a farmyard is a place on a farm.

More to think about

1. Copy these root words. Add two more words that use the same root word.

   a) day – to**day** **day**light   b) rain

   c) snow   d) some

   e) wind   f) water

2. Write five sentences each using one of the words you added, like this:

   When I woke up this morning the **daylight** was streaming through the curtains.

Now try these

Join the prefixes and suffixes in the box to the root words. Make as many words as you can.

ly	un	ful	able	al

love	perfect	wise	sure
fair	correct	most	help

Diminutives

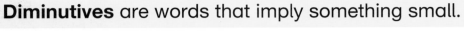

Diminutives are words that imply something small.

a **mini**-market
(a small shop)

an eag**let**
(a small eagle)

Sometimes diminutives are made by adding a **prefix**.

Sometimes diminutives are made by adding a **suffix**.

Practice

Copy these words. Join each with its diminutive form.

1. eagle	owlet
2. cod	bullock
3. duck	kitten
4. goose	eaglet
5. bull	duckling
6. lamb	codling
7. owl	lambkin
8. cat	gosling

More to think about

Write the correct definitions with the diminutives.

1. statuette   a small kitchen

2. kitchenette   a small stream

3. mini-series   a small drop of liquid

4. droplet   a small ornamental figure

5. nestling   a short series

6. streamlet   a small piece of food

7. morsel   a young bird, still in the nest

Now try these

1. Choose the correct ending to use to complete each diminutive.

| let | kin | icle | ette | el | ling | et |

a) cigar_____   b) nap_____

c) book_____   d) sap_____

e) cygn_____   f) cub_____

g) satch_____

> Use a dictionary to help if necessary.

2. Now write a definition for each word.

Using its and it's

When do you use **its** or **it's**?

It's with an apostrophe stands for **it is** or **it has**.

Its means **belonging to**.

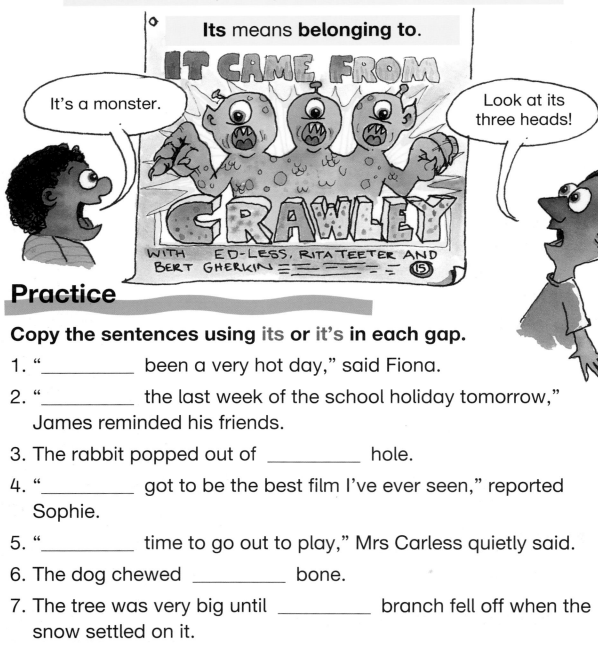

It's a monster.

Look at its three heads!

Practice

Copy the sentences using its or it's in each gap.

1. "_____ been a very hot day," said Fiona.

2. "_____ the last week of the school holiday tomorrow," James reminded his friends.

3. The rabbit popped out of _____ hole.

4. "_____ got to be the best film I've ever seen," reported Sophie.

5. "_____ time to go out to play," Mrs Carless quietly said.

6. The dog chewed _____ bone.

7. The tree was very big until _____ branch fell off when the snow settled on it.

More to think about

Copy the passage. Choose its or it's to fill each gap.

A trip to the beach

"_____ been a terrible day," the family agreed as they drove home in their car. It had all started in the morning when Mum said, " _____ a lovely day and the sun is out. Let's go to the beach."
Once they arrived Dad said, "_____ got to be the busiest I've ever seen!" A dog ran up and shook _____ wet body all over them.
The children ran into the sea, nearly stepping on a crab. It snapped _____ claws. Suddenly dark clouds covered the sky.
"_____ raining," called Mum. "Quick, _____ time to get out of the water."
They jumped in the car soaking wet, but… "Oh, no! _____ not going to start. _____ out of petrol!" they all groaned.
Two hours later they were finally on their way home.

Now try these

1. Write four sentences using **its**.

2. Write four sentences using **it's**.

it's *its* its
its *it's*
it's **its** it's

Progress Test B

1. Copy these nouns. Write whether each one is masculine (m) or feminine (f).

   a) princess (f)   b) husband
   c) bride   d) niece
   e) brother   f) uncle
   g) wife   h) son

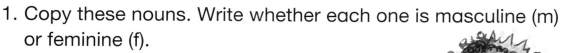

2. These pairs of words have got joined together. Separate them. Write each pair.

   a) m u s i c a l t o g e t h e r = musical altogether
   b) tropicalways   c) historicalmost
   d) signalright   e) accidentalthough
   f) comicalmighty   g) medicalso

3. Copy the table. Write each word in the box in the correct column.

helicopter	farthing	computer	hark	video
robot	monocle	cinders	television	radar
	breeches	bonnet		

Newer words	Older words
helicopter	farthing

4. Copy this story. Underline all the **ight** words.

In the <u>night</u> I saw a <u>bright</u> <u>light</u>
right in the middle of the woods.
I felt frightened so I held my torch
tightly. What a sight! In a clearing
I saw two knights having a fight!

5. Copy these words. Take the suffix off each word.
   Write the word you are left with.

   a) washable – wash
   b) personal
   c) helpful
   d) poisonous
   e) girlish
   f) watery
   g) comforting
   h) poetic

6. Copy these sets of words. Underline the odd word out
   in each set.
   a) cone, bone, <u>gone</u>
   b) cow, low, mow
   c) sweat, beat, heat
   d) hood, blood, good
   e) police, twice, rice
   f) cost, post, most

7. Copy these words. Join them to make compound words.

book	brush
pen	cake
tooth	knife
fire	bag
tea	board
pan	shoe
horse	case
card	work

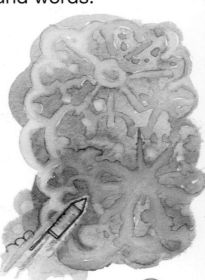

8. Write the words in Set B that have the same root words as those in Set A.
   Underline the root word like this: dis<u>comfort</u>, <u>comfort</u>er

Set A	shopkeeper unfriendly powerful action cleanest misunderstand

Set B	friendliness understandable cleanly actor empower shopping

9. Copy and complete each sentence.

A duckling is a small _____.

A kitten is a small _____.

An owlet is a small _____.

An eaglet is a small _____.

A gosling is a small _____.

10. Copy the sentences. Choose **it's** or **its** to complete each one.

   a) The dragon blew smoke from _____ mouth.

   b) _____ a lovely day today.

   c) My dog has lost _____ lead.

   d) I know _____ here somewhere!

   e) Can't you see that _____ been ripped?

   f) The fire engine raced down the street with _____ siren going.